I0412780

Abortion Is Not
An Option

Abortion Is Not An Option

Melanie D.G. Howard

Copyright © 2012 by Melanie D.G. Howard.

ISBN: Softcover   978-1-4691-7394-8
             Hardcover   978-1-4771-0658-7

All rights reserved. No part of this book may be reproduced or transmitted in any form or by any means, electronic or mechanical, including photocopying, recording, or by any information storage and retrieval system, without permission in writing from the copyright owner.

This book was printed in the United States of America.

To order additional copies of this book, contact:
Xlibris Corporation
1-888-795-4274
www.Xlibris.com
Orders@Xlibris.com
56957

Dedication

This book is dedicated to the memory of the late Bishop D. Lee Owens, who released me into the gospel ministry and taught me to honor God by rendering the gifts He's given me back to Him in service: and to Dr. J. Lemuel Spence for advocating the progress to transport me into my next.

I also dedicate this work to my shero; the most wonderful mother in the world, Evelyn H. Harper. Thank you for believing in me enough to impel me, and to invest so very much in me. I am especially grateful to my god-sisters; Shellye, for the material to work with and Louise, for allowing me to complete the process.

Thank you to my beautiful children: Chanica & Brandon Owens, Takiyya Green, and Lenard & Laura Howard for your unconditional love. To my god-children and spiritual children: thank you for encouraging me to go for it and share my gifts with the world.

Thank you to the greatest church ever, The Temple of Praise and Worship for trusting the God in me.

Contents

Abortion Is Not An Option

(Introduction)

God has a purpose

Sometimes we may wonder why, even though certain things happen there are particular thoughts that still come to mind repeatedly. No matter what we go through, no matter how we go through it, we just can't shake these colorful leaves out of the tree of our mind. Trials come, and tribulations go, and yet many dreams and visions remain in tact. Our dreams and visions, as God's children, are often tied to the plan and purpose He has for our lives. He connected them to our minds before we were born and fastens our every experience to them like pieces of a puzzle to form a complete portrait.

You may expend plenty of time spinning around in different directions, trying to escape from your past or from your future. It doesn't matter what course you take, when God has a purpose for you there is virtually no escape. God is not in the habit of doing things arbitrarily. He has a plan and purpose for each of our lives. His plan is not contingent on where you come from, what you've experienced in life, or who you do or do not know. Nothing else matters when God has a purpose. He's already stated that He has a particular plan for you.[1] In other words, the only plan that makes a difference is the one He desires to be executed.

What it is, you ask, that leads us to the plan of the Almighty? When you understand and receive the fact that God has a purpose, you must open your mind to the pregnant possibilities within that purpose and plan.

---

[1]   For I know the thoughts and plans that I have for you, says the Lord, thoughts and plans for welfare and peace and not for evil, to give you hope in your final outcome. (Jeremiah 29:11)

Everything God does is very pointed; He knows the end before we get to the beginning. Since we have the ability to make choices, there are many prospects that could occur, contingent on our focus. God said, "I place before you death and life, I would that you choose life."[2] The Lord has a desire for each one of us, but He gives us the opportunity to decide whether we want what He wants. We should remember that He also said, "No one who puts his hand to the plow and looks back is fit for the kingdom of God."[3] There are some facets in life that once we have been exposed to them we find it not so easy to walk away.

a·bor·tion: *1)* Cessation of normal growth, especially of an organ or other body part, prior to full development or maturation. *2)* Something malformed or incompletely developed; a monstrosity.

Abortion as we know it deals with disabling the possibility of full-term healthy birth usually concerning a child. When the child is removed from the womb prematurely, the fact that they are not fully developed causes deformities or death. Many women chose to have an abortion because they are not prepared or willing to accept the changes childbirth will bring in their life. Another reason a woman may have an abortion may be that an unwanted or unintentional situation lead to the pregnancy.

As we deal with spiritual situations the term abortion represents the lack of ability to follow through with and operate in the ministry assignment God has called you to. We have to go through certain processes and make progress to develop into the prophets, priests, and kings we were ordained in our mother's womb to be. Development is not always easy. Excelling in any area of life can be quite challenging; nevertheless it is necessary that we press through these challenges to evolve into our true selves.

---

2   I call heaven and earth to witness this day against you that I have set before you life and death, the blessings and the curses; therefore choose life, that you and your descendants may live: (Deuteronomy 30:19)

3   Jesus said to him, No one who puts his hand to the plow and looks back [to the things behind] is fit for the kingdom of God. (Luke 9:62)

What do you do when in the middle of performing a powerful task, things get tough? How do you handle it when you find yourself in danger on behalf of another? As it is in the natural, so it is also in the spiritual. Removing ones self from the plan of God prematurely will cause you to be spiritually deformed, or the impending danger of spiritual death. Sometimes we feel that we are not prepared to handle the changes associated with whole-heartedly serving God. We often find that His plan is not at all what we would have thought it to be. Your choice may come down to whether you decide to go through and save others or quit, saving yourself.

This book entertains the thought that the choices we make in life definitely affect others. A woman may find herself to be impregnated with a child she did not want. Just so—the people of God may find themselves to be inseminated with spiritual gifts they didn't essentially long for. In either case the outcome is ultimately shaped by the decision made.

Let's examine the circumstances Jesus allowed to influence the decisions He made on the way to the cross. How do those decisions affect us now? What other examples are found in the word of God to help us in taking the correct route in deciding if we should weather the storms connected to our purpose? The discussion of destiny has been aroused in the body of Christ with a newfound vehemence. What we apparently do not consider is the cost of the pursuit of destiny. If we are to reach any destination, we have to commit and then hold to that commitment throughout the journey. You cannot abort the process of any pursuit and expect to obtain the full satisfaction that comes with completion.

Have You Been Turned On?

Chapter 1 John 3:1-21[i]

Life is made up of experiences, courses of events and activities. There are good experiences in which you may learn something or gain something. This could occur in a classroom, boardroom, a living room, or no room at all. The possibility exists that such an experience could come from a spoken word. A word, fitly spoken, can catapult you into destiny. It can present a pivotal point, shifting you from failure to success. And we find that a word, when it's for you, has the most awesome precision in timing, tact, and grace for your ability to receive it. Your word has to come from just the right person, someone who is able to capture your attention. This could be an authority figure, a family member, friend, or anyone called to minister the word of God to masses of people. Everyone cannot deliver the word you need at the time you need it. Each experience presented by verbal inclination has to have the ability to move the recipient from one posture to another. Nonetheless, if the word is for you at the particular time it is delivered something seems to leap on the inside of you as if to notify you that it's for you. It may cause your heart to pound, your ears to wiggle, your eye to twitch, or your feet to tap. There must be a connection to a right now word; a witness in your spirit. You can then apply whatever you receive from the word so it would provide for you a better way of living.

Just as there are good experiences, there are bad ones. The bad experiences are the ones that make you weary. These are the situations that pull on your heart-strings, causing great pains and strains. It's hard to imagine that a negative experience could possibly lead us to a glorious destiny. Even at the end of the journey the proprietor might find it hard to connect meager beginnings with a prosperous crescendo. There have been many times when God used a not so great situation to get someone to the blessing that was waiting for them. In the book of Genesis, Joseph dreams a dream that seems to indicate that he would be sitting on top of the world with people serving him.[4] What Joseph's dream did not reveal to him was the route he would have to take to get to the top. He certainly did not realize this journey was to begin in a pit. What would land him in the place he had visualized would be presented in such a miraculous way that if told in advance about it, even he probably wouldn't have believed it. He never would have imagined that interpreting a dream in the dungeon of a jail would align him for the palace, but that's exactly what happened.

Then there are the experiences that are very ugly. These situations sometimes have lifetime trauma connected to them. Our ugly experiences bring about damaging consequences and dangerous crises, which maneuver through our mental, emotional, and physical transports causing great anxiety. How could a lifetime sentence possibly result in a plateau of palace exploits? With God all things are possible. He has great plans for His people, which began before we were even born. He says in Jeremiah 29:11 that there is a plan, a thought or expectation that would lead to a positive ending.[5] We therefore must trust in the God who has the plan, knowing that we are always in His thoughts. He is able to bring to pass the absolute best out of the overall worse inauguration.

No matter where you are in life at this moment, if you yield your way of doing things to God's desire for you He can handle every thing: the good, the bad, the ugly, and even the great. When you live totally connected to His will the divine plan that was already appointed to you can be revealed to and even through you.

The Realization

There was a man named Nicodemus. The Bible says he was a ruler of the Jews. Nicodemus came to talk to Jesus because he had a need and believed Jesus was the one who could address his need. Although this man had houses, power, and money, he still had an issue that needed to be dealt with. He had authority over people, and influence. But there was

---

4 Genesis 37:1-41:46

5 Jer 29:11 For I know the thoughts that I think toward you, saith the LORD, thoughts of peace, and not of evil, to give you an expected end.

something missing in his life. This simply goes to show that no matter what kind of earthly possessions or power you may have, there are some issues that can only be answered by God. The fact that Nicodemus came to Jesus by night, some would consider an act of caution. It's amazing that this man would come to the Lord with his problem, but then not want anyone else to know it.

Nicodemus was a Pharisee. The Pharisees were bitter toward Jesus, and persistent in their desire to destroy his influence over the Jewish people. They were an arrogant sect of Jews; therefore it was unusual for a man such as this to seek out the Messiah with sincerity and humility. This would have been seen as a sign of weakness for a great man who was a ruler of the Jews. Nicodemus had heard about Jesus, he had even seen some of His works with his own eyes. His curiosity was aroused, and he now had a burning desire like he had never dealt with before.

So often we find ourselves in predicaments that for one reason or another, we may not want to share with others. It might be that you were a prostitute who would rather avoid the judgments of those who dare to act as if they have never done any wrong. Maybe it's a drug habit that is best kept secret and not put on display. Possibly it's alcoholism that stems back for three generations. Perhaps you may think those around you wouldn't understand your sudden divorce, due to the affair that you had no responsibility in. The fact of the matter is that we, like Nicodemus, often feel a need to protect our reputation, and not taint whatever level of respect we have. There are just some situations we'd simply rather not share with others, escaping the misinterpretation, or misunderstanding of man. Some conversations are for God's ear only.

The Reception

Now that the encounter was real, there was the matter of what to do with the answer he heard. Jesus had answered Nicodemus' question plainly and clearly. There's nothing like receiving an answer to a burning question. When the Lord answers the question, the ball is then in your court…what you do with the answer is up to you. You then have a choice: will you follow through so you can benefit from doing what He told you, or will you back down and leave things the way they were before your divine experience?

If you seek an answer to a question one thing you should remember is that you must then be in a posture to receive an answer. So often we are not receptive of the answer to the very question we asked. It could be that we were not prepared for the change required in order to realize the fullness of the promised treasure. Maybe what we are scheduled to receive is not quite what we bargained for. Possibly the cost is too high and we don't want to pay. Some people opt to remain typical, rather than do what it takes to reach the divine plateau of true purpose for their life.

Belief is all that's really required to be able to receive from God. All you need is faith as your ticket to put you in the exchange line. You can then exchange that faith ticket to take possession of your promise. The bible tells us that; "Faith gives us an air of hope concerning things promised, but are not yet in our sight."[6ii] You must be able to see the unseen. That unseen thing must then have such an effect on you that you can act upon it, although you cannot see it. All of the circumstances around you may look completely opposite of what the Lord said, yet you have something to hold on to…that ticket obtained from the word that was spoken. The spoken word has power that is so profound that not any other force can combat what that word means in the spirit realm.

The Redeemed

If you've been turned on, it means that you've been redeemed: delivered from the curse of the law of sin. Even though you may wake up with a question, go to work with a question, have lunch with a question, drive home with a question, or even still have a burning question throughout the evening time, there is an answer for you. There is an answer that is so profound, yet so very simple. There is an answer that cannot come out of Harvard, Stanford, or Yale. You can't pay a psychiatrist or psychologist for it. The psychic hotline can't conjure it up, the gambler can't roll it out, and the anthropologist can't dig it up. This is the answer Nicodemus sought. The amazing thing was that he sought the answer from the supreme source.

---

6   Now faith is the substance of things hoped for, the evidence of things not seen. (Heb 11:1)

"Jesus answered and said unto him, Verily, verily, I say unto thee, Except a man be born again, he cannot see the kingdom of God." (John 3:3) In order to receive what God has for you, you must first be born again. Everything new begins with a birthing process; a commencement from what was old is a step into something new. Jesus came to serve as a form of mid-wife so those of us who once could not imagine ourselves in the beloved family of God would be positioned as 'joint heirs with Christ'. He came to dwell in this earth to seek those of us who were lost, lacking direction, without opportunity to know what its like to be in His presence for a moment. It had been established that we would be with Him throughout eternity. However, this left Nicodemus yet with a question: maybe he missed something in the answer as it was given, but he couldn't understand how it might be possible that a man who was fully grown would be born a second time.[7]

How was it possible that an educated man like Nicodemus could stand before Jesus the Christ, the anointed one and the anointing, and not have a clue about something that should be so very clear? We would have to liken him to many of us. God inspired men to read His word. So many of us can read it and miss uncomplicated truths. Although man may only be able to understand processes such a birthing in a natural sense, God is connected to that which is spiritual because He is a Spirit. So there was a breakdown in communication between a holy Christ and a carnal Pharisee. We can only walk into what God has for us by His Spirit. Jesus told Nicodemus that man must be born of the water which is natural, and by the Spirit which is indeed spiritual. The first birth (water) connects us to man, but the second birth (spirit) connects us to God.

---

[7]   Nicodemus saith unto him, How can a man be born when he is old? can he enter the second time into his mother's womb, and be born? (Joh 3:4)

Lay it all on the Line

To do the will of God, to bring forth what He desires, can only come out of total surrender. God takes no pleasure in partial commitment. Many of us only want to yield the exterior or noticeable things to Him. We like for people to think we've got it going on in our relationship to God. It's like a husband and wife putting on airs in front of others, when in fact they haven't gotten along since who knows when. They may seem to be the perfect couple to outsiders, but if we could follow them home we might find a relationship hanging on by a mere thread. If we were to take an honest assessment one would have to admit that there are habits, situations, and selfish desires still present in our lives which are there because we simply have not been ready to give them up. How many times has there been someone in deliverance service determined not to give up their devilish ways: everybody praying and (whaling) over them, calling on the Lord to take away the very thing they don't want to give up.

Some habits are easily broken while others are so much a part of us that they create a much greater challenge. We may even wonder who we might be if not for what we know to be part of us. It is not a matter of whether we know God wants us to walk away from practicing these bad habits; we may have read in the word what He specifically says about it or where the principle is mentioned. As children of God, we should lay these habits before Him and walk away from them, trusting Him to give us the stamina necessary to deny ourselves and not pick them up again. There's an old hymn that asks a very pertinent question: "Is your all on the altar of sacrifice laid?" In other words, have you laid everything on the altar? God wants to handle all of your issues; but He will only take away what you give to Him and walk away from.

We don't always have control over the situations we face in life, but what we do have is control over what place we allow life's situations to take. Too often we allow situations to become our driving force instead of forcing the situation out of our direct path. Situations appear in different forms and are not always, of themselves, negative. The obstacle is not always in what the situation is, but sometimes is found in the affect it has on you. If you've found yourself without a job, for instance, you can either sit around whining about not having that job or get up and go after the next great thing God has for you. You may have had to deal with a loss of relationship. Your choices are to sit and cry about that old relationship or move on with life and remain open for a new and lasting relationship. (You never know what worse situation or circumstance the Lord rescued you from). When we find ourselves going through many of the changes in life we have to prepare ourselves, gird up our loins, and most of all—trust God. He knows what will best serve you in the plans He has for your life.

On His way to the cross, Jesus found himself at a point to consider the fullness of the effect of the consequences tied to whatever decision He would make. He took an honest look at what His choices were, and the bearing each one would have on not only the chosen people but those who stood the possibility of being adopted into the royal family of God. The direction He took would express what was most important; the lives of men that He was born to save, or His own life. The ultimate question Jesus had to entertain was if He was willing to lay His very life on the line. This is the determining factor to consider as we navigate through the process of fulfilling our life's purpose. If indeed it is our resolution to do the will of the Lord, we must do it vehemently, without wavering.

Surrender your Pleasure

An amazing fact is that one cannot please God and take pleasure in his own will at the same time. This, of course, means that at times we have to give up our own desire, and give in to His desire for our life. What a disturbing thought in the naturally selfish mind of man this can be. We are known to expend much of our energy trying to find some way, any way, to put a spin on our current situation so it would suit the ideal outcome we imagine. If there is any way to get the things we want most in life, that is what we can be found seeking. Maybe if we could play the lottery, win a drawing, or just wish it into being, life would be so much better than the suffering of this very moment. The question is, would any of this guarantee better or more productive life? Would it really please God for me to win fast money? Could I manage quick fortune? The truth of the matter is that God desires great things for His children, but we must remember that there is a process that sets us on the God-ordained path of prosperity.[8] It is His pleasure that will lead us to prosperity; and the prosperity we gain will reach much further than our bank account.[9] This prosperity speaks of the eternal future: a future that goes beyond anything in human imagination.

As our hearts are turned to God, we develop an awesome aspiration to please Him. Before I reached that pinnacle of understanding His truest desire, my focus was on myself and I only did what pleased my flesh. Once I crossed over the threshold of spiritual realization I traded my carnal egocentricity for the spiritual observance of grace to walk out the path that was set before me. This new attitude helped me to persevere when I found myself in the deepest of valley experiences in life. In the midst of the struggle when a decision had to be made, the yoke was now easy. Whereas my past offered man-made broken promises, my future was filled with good and perfect gifts. Every day would not be happy for me. In fact, there were more challenges ahead, but I now had a promise from God that whatever the future held would work to finish that work He had begun in me.[10]

I'd rather please God and allow Him to finish the desired work in my life, sending a sweet aroma into His nostrils than to disappoint Him with the stench of sin. Moses could have lived the good life. He had been raised as the son of Pharaoh, the heir to his throne. But God had a different plan for Moses' life. He would be given the charge to go to the throne of Egypt and instruct Pharaoh to release the chosen nation of God. What an overwhelming task to have conferred upon any one man.

---

8   For it is God who worketh in you both to will and to work, for his good pleasure. (Php 2:13)

9   Beloved, I pray that in all things thou mayest prosper and be in health, even as thy soul prospereth. (3Jn 1:2)

10   Being confident of this very thing, that he who began a good work in you will perfect it until the day of Jesus Christ: (Php 1:6)

As Moses discussed the weight of his task and his fear of rejection with the Lord, he was introduced to the assistants who would be with him and the weapons to be utilized during this executive meeting. The most powerful thing was that he was never charged to go out and purchase new equipment, but rather was directed to use what he already had to accomplish the directive specified.

Moses took his assistants and marched in to Pharaoh with the command to release the people of God. When (Pharaoh) laughed at the man of God and resisted the order, Moses followed the instructions he was given to persuade him. Pharaoh had no choice but to yield to the demonstration of the power of God. Pharaoh was the most powerful man in Egypt; owning all of the land. He was also the High Priest of the Temple and represented the pagan gods. (Pharaoh: Lord of Two Lands) These pagan/earthly gods were no match for Jehovah: the Lord of lords, who created the earth and everything in it. Ultimately, it could be said that Moses had to decide, moment by moment, between following the God who created the earth or give in to fear of gods within the earth. As with Moses, you have to decide whether to live in fear of the powers in the earth or stand in faith against them in trust of the God who rules heaven and earth. When you follow the order of the Almighty God, surrendering and submitting to His will, you will see how greatness flows through you. We are not able to do much in and of ourselves, but much can happen by allowing the omnipotence of Jehovah to work through us. (You may have to give up what you temporarily believe to be pleasurable in order to get to some very permanent possibilities.) Remember, He has sight of the end and you have no idea what to lies ahead. [11]

Although Jesus had resolved to yield all other options to His true assignment, He knew that to do so would only allow the Father to exhibit His actual plan for man in the complete scheme of this maneuver: the proof that He is our Jehovah. Had He not gone to the cross, we would not have the benefit of exact revelation of the provision we are privileged to be partakers of.

---

[11] There is a way which seemeth right unto a man; But the end thereof are the ways of death. (Pro 14:12)

Steer God's Provision

God is a provider. His name, Jehovah Jireh, means The Lord my Provider. If you have a need to be met, any need, no matter how deep, He is able to provide. So often people wonder, if God is so great and wants us to have good things, why would He allow us to suffer without. Why would a God who knows all things and to whom all things belong not give His children what they need? In my observation, more often than not our needs are not met simply because we have not asked the Lord for provision. Before you say anything, yes He does know what we need. It is still very necessary to state your need and trust Him to meet the need. There are, however, a few reasons why we often do not trust our needs to the hand of the one we know is able to handle them.

One of the greatest issues we have with asking God to meet our need is that although we say we love and trust Him, our perception is limited to what is before our eyes. As carnal beings, the tendency for us is that we attempt to deal with all of our concerns from the perspective we recognize. This being the case, we look to the wrong sources for answers. For instance, if there is a financial need…the first thought is to work a second job or maybe borrow from someone, making ourselves slaves to those who have which is definitely not the will of God for His own.[12]

Another method of dealing with need is that we pray about it. Sounds like the right thing to do, right? The only problem with this is we don't actually relinquish our problems to God. We have the power to steer the power of God to work on our behalf. If you are going to steer His power to work for you, you must first be willing to yield control of all things to the omnipotent one.[13] When we call on the name of the Lord, He hears us, and He will answer us. The power of God is at our disposal. I

---

[12]   The rich ruleth over the poor; And the borrower is servant to the lender. (Pro 22:7)

[13]   Now unto him that is able to do exceeding abundantly above all that we ask or think, according to the power that worketh in us, Unto him *be* glory in the church by Christ Jesus throughout all ages, world without end. Amen. (Eph 3:20-21)

dare say, if it is not working in your life it would most likely be because you are not tapping into it. You have access to everything He has, but remember that you may only use this power when you operate in the spirit realm. This brings us to another issue to consider: our proclivity to tell God how to answer us with the expectation that He is to obey us. The creator is not subject to the created. We should seek His desire for our life, and then be open to receive the answer from Him and take His instructions. The spirit must rule over the flesh, as we are created in His image; that is, we were created spiritual beings that are exposed to a natural living experience.

What many people who claim to be God's children have apparently missed along the way is that we have the ability to steer His provision. The way we do this is through our expectation. We invoke the power of the Lord to move when we acknowledge that His desire is not for any of His children to go lacking. The Father is pleased any time we demonstrate our trust in Him. The only way to demonstrate the level of trust we have is by asking for something, and expecting that need to be met. A child who would ask their parent for what they need definitely shows that they have an inherent belief that mom or dad can handle the weight of their need and that He is able to provide. God wants us to prove that we know He is able to give us what we need by asking for it, and thereby giving Him the opportunity to render unto us what we request.

Anticipating an unjust death by hanging could not sway the one who knew this to be the only way to provoke God to move in the sovereignty of His perfect will for man. Jesus Christ stated that there was purposed even in this horrible fate. The necessity of the cross had to do with redemption of God's chosen people as well as any other man who would select to receive the process and the processor as their means of eternal security. We have the power to steer the provision of God in a direction that will leave us scuttling around for ways of fulfillment, or in direction to not only allow, but to invoke Him to fulfill His pledge to us.

Summon up God's Promise

No matter what happens in your life, I hope you remember one thing, God keeps every promise He makes. He will not lie. He cannot lie.[14] He is a faithful God and will do what he promised. He is the ultimate promise keeper. Man may make a promise and go back on it. The person you trust most in life is subject to renege on a promise they've made, but Jehovah is none of those persons. Whatever He has said He would do, we can trust that it will come to pass.

The only thing you have to do to get God to move is to call on Him to do what He said; trusting and believing that He is faithful and just to perform every promise. A summons is a writ of request, an appeal.[15] God is not moved by nervousness and anxiety. He's not going to show up just because you're freaked out over circumstances or situations. Whatever you're going through, you need to stop focusing on it and remember His promise not to walk out on you.[16] You don't have to worry about anything; you already have a promise of God. In fact, you should walk as if the promise has already been realized.

A millionaire doesn't act the same as a person who is wishing for or hoping to come into one hundred dollars. The person who has walks like he has, even when he struggles to maintain. Ultimately, if God's people would live each day as if our godly promises are in tact, our outward expression would be that of royalty and not as paupers. Believe God and He will bring it to pass.

There was promise connected to the haunting Calvary occurrence. The only way for the promise to be manifested was for innocent blood to

---

[14]   God *is* not a man, that he should lie; neither the son of man, that he should repent: hath he said, and shall he not do *it?* or hath he spoken, and shall he not make it good? (Num 23:19)

[15]   Be careful for nothing; but in every thing by prayer and supplication with thanksgiving let your requests be made known unto God. (Php 4:6)

[16]   *Let your* conversation *be* without covetousness; *and be* content with such things as ye have: for he hath said, I will never leave thee, nor forsake thee. (Heb 13:5)

be shed on the cross. Many have found fault with those who chose to release Barabbas and crucify Jesus. The problem with this attitude is that the life of Barabbas had no value except he would be spared as opposed to the Lamb of God. The promise given was divinely attributed to the agreement that Jesus the Christ, though He had done no wrong, would endure the destiny of achievement to this excruciating demise.

Something to Hold On To

Chapter 3 (Work With what you've Got)/Psalm 31:9-15[iv]

"I have a call on my life. I do recognize that God has called me to do a great work. The problem I'm having now is that although there is a certainty about the work to be done, I am completely ill-equipped to fulfill the mandate of my call. I don't think I can live up to the expectations of being perfect. People in church are funny and I certainly don't have what it takes to deal with the challenges I've seen other ministers cope with." These words have been spoken too often by people who claim to love the Lord and want to please Him.

Men and women all over the globe have faced the issue of dealing with a call they feel they are not be able to carry out. Many have run away from what they know they have to do because of spiritual immaturity, low self-esteem, and the lack of understanding as to how to make it happen. Several questions come to mind: What will it take to completely work the work He assigned to my hands? Am I qualified to do this particular work? How can I prepare to do this? What gifts do I have, or what gifts are essential to walk this all the way through? God requires that above all we would have a willing spirit and a heart to obey Him.

You may think initially that you may have to stack up credentials, or learn some new tricks to do what you've been called to do. Whereas education is a definite an asset, the only thing required to begin your journey of fulfillment is to use what you already have. The greatest thing I considered was whether I would be received or heard by the people I was called to minister to. Recognition of the very fact that there was a higher call on my life brought me to a place where my own weakness was first brought before me. Anyone who is truly serious about a call that sets them before others to preach the perfect gospel of the Lord

Jesus Christ has to examine himself before there can be any possibility of preparedness to approach anyone else.

The process of examining one's self may bring about excruciating realities that must be dealt with, but it gives us to the power we need to conduct the work. Just like David, we have to first ask for God's mercy. We must ask for mercy because of the many sins we have committed, among other things. Our sinful ways cause much trouble; this makes the work of mercy necessary. Sin reveals trouble, which reveals weakness and helps us understand why mercy is required.

Revelation of sin also brings to the forefront the many persons you may minister to who knew you when. We all used to be something; everyone is an 'ex' something or other, and somewhere along the line we had onlookers of those experiences. Some of our witnesses are there to support the new direction we've taken now that our spiritual life has become more valuable to us. However, there are always those who do not appreciate nor support us in this newness of life.

David stated that he was a reproach not only to those who were against him, but more so to those who were in support of him. Knowledge of who we were and what we used to do gives room for criticism. Open sin is an embarrassment to the body of Christ. It is imperative for us to confront the sin in our lives, especially those of us who minister the gospel to others. What makes it so important is, if it has been dealt with there is no room for contamination of the glorious message that we preach. David in the 31st Psalm[17] was confronting what he knew would be a detriment to his witness and hinders the ability of others to believe in the power of the Almighty God that worked in him. While he acknowledged that his grief was directly connected to his own sins, he knew there was solace in trusting God to bring him to his expected end.

---

[17] Have mercy upon me, O LORD, for I am in trouble: mine eye is consumed with grief, *yea,* my soul and my belly. For my life is spent with grief, and my years with sighing: my strength faileth because of mine iniquity, and my bones are consumed. I was a reproach among all mine enemies, but especially among my neighbours, and a fear to mine acquaintance: they that did see me without fled from me. (Psa 31:9-11)

The control of his life remained committed to the Creator of heaven, earth, sky, and man.

Hearing the negative perspective of men and women around you can create a world of stress and pain. Some of our sin was committed in pleasantry. Maybe you were a partier, did a few drugs, lead a life of promiscuity. You may have been the life of the party, telling jokes and cursing or even calling people out of their name as a means of entertainment; walking away without bruising anyone, or so you thought anyway. Unfortunately, for many of us, we left painful tracks that would humiliate us now if discovered.

The devil is called the accuser of the saints: that is, his job description calls for him to throw your troubles and issues back in your face at the most perturbing moment. He lay in wait for you to get to the most public situation so he may expose your most damaging secrets. This tactic is not new at all; it has been used since the beginning of time. The humiliation of it all can make you feel less than competent to accomplish your special work. The challenge our past lives can present is observed in the position we now walk in, commanding that we preach against the very acts we've committed. "How could I preach against what I have partaken in with a clear conscious?"

You don't want to be ignored because of where you stem from. Certainly God can get no glory from a word spoken that dissipates in the air. The word must be spread throughout the earth; and if there is a call on your life, it's to take hold of the plow and cover your area of the world with the gospel message so that souls might be saved and won to the body of Christ. No matter who may attempt to hinder the gospel by slandering your name, if you have confessed the sin in your life and repented of it the path is cleared for you to do what you're called to do. God never intended for you to try to be someone else, or hide from who you are to spread the gospel. You have to use what you've got. Whatever sins you've committed, they can be valuable tools in your effort to work in the Lord's vineyard.

A prostitute can receive the message and witness of someone who has been delivered from prostitution. A pimp is more willing to listen to someone who has once maneuvered in the same alleyways he's done business in. A drug addict is likely to be open to receive from another who is prepared to admit that they have at some point walked the same course. Therefore we benefit by trusting God above all. We can trust Him to cover us. He will uphold us in the very face of those who would dare persecute, or attempt to shut us up.

The fact is, if our motive is to please God, there is a force within us that will not allow us to be quieted. We might try to walk away but the power and call of God will arrest us. Before we were even born a mechanism was placed inside us that cause us to feel that we have no other choice but to preach the word of God. It doesn't matter where we find ourselves; we have the responsibility of telling those that we meet along the way about the God of mercy and grace. Just continue to trust that your life is in the hand of the omnipotent God. He will supply everything you need to do what you're called to do.

Start with what you have and work with that. God asked Moses what he had in his hand. He replied, only a rod. God showed him how the rod could be used to get his message across to Pharaoh. The same way He desired Moses to learn how to use the tool he already had, He wants you to know you're equipped to fulfill your calling. Your life experiences have prepared you to walk out this vocation. The enemy tried to convince you that the road you've walked had disqualified you, but on the contrary, the past has given you credentials to handle the road ahead. We can't afford to listen to the enemy, especially since we are aware that he knows what we're called to do. Don't spend valuable time falling into his traps. Move beyond this and focus on working through who you are in Christ.

Whatever you are called to do, it should be done with great zeal. Make sure you are pleasing God, not pleasing man, and certainly not pleasing the enemy. Put all of your hope and trust in the one true God who is able to keep you in all of your ways. He is the one who called you. He is also the one who will keep you. Whatever He has equipped you with is more than enough to fulfill the call on your life. It doesn't mean the way will be made easy, but it does mean you will be able to work through it.

We may often wonder to ourselves: can I make it through the roughest moments in life? Is there a roadmap that will lead me to a place of acceptance? When you look in the mirror, who or what's looking back at you? In the most troubled times it doesn't even seem like you have what it takes to get out of your own tight spot. You know you can't help anyone else when you don't know how to dig yourself out of a deep, dark hole. But God's people must walk by faith, trusting that you can make it through your most trying times. While you're going through, focus on what God desires to teach you in the midst of the trial. He always has a plan with a desired end. If you go through a wilderness situation, just know that you should come out better than you went in, no matter what it looks like or how you feel.

As Jesus got closer to His purpose walk He became very sorrowful. According to the writings in the gospels, immediately after what is now known as the Last Supper, He retreated to the place where He normally went to pray known as the garden of Gethsemane. It's interesting that the closer He got to the place of prayer the more sorrowful He became. Jesus knew there was something horrific that He was about to face right at the place of prayer. He would soon be betrayed by one of His very own disciples. This would set Him on the path of the fulfillment of the extraordinary purpose for which He was born. Bearing the cross (load) of Christ is sometimes sorrowful as the people closest to you may not support you in your quest to fulfill your calling. You must bear this weight of sorrow just as Christ did no matter who willingly stands with you. The ability to press on with limited to no carnal support says to God that He can trust you with the next task of your assignment, and catapults you to the next realm: enabling you to reach the mark and receive your reward.

God placed purpose in you before you were ever born. The Lord speaks this to Jeremiah in the first chapter of the so-named book.[18] While some are running after what they assume to be their godly purpose in the earth, many of us have had what we considered good reason to desire anything else in the world but to do what He called us to do. In this

---

[18]   Before I formed thee in the belly I knew thee; and before thou camest forth out of the womb I sanctified thee, *and* I ordained thee a prophet unto the nations. (Jer 1:5)

dialogue with God, He shares with Jeremiah that he has reason to press on in spite of what others may think. Whether he understood it or not, he had not just received a call; it was there all of the time. Like Jesus, he now had something to hold on to…he didn't choose his calling: he was chosen for the calling. He was anointed to handle all stresses connected to it.

We don't get to choose our calling: we are chosen for the calling. When you have been chosen by God to do a work every experience in your life has occurred to prepare you to walk out your purpose. Jesus became sorrowful because he knew the magnitude of what He was about to face. Jeremiah was nervous about whether the people were going to listen to someone who was so young. Those of us who truly understand the full virtue of what is expected of us may be uneasy about it. Like Jeremiah, our reasons are usually very different from those of Jesus, who knew the pain He was about to endure. Most of us understand that as we have potential to succeed, we have just as much potential to fail. Not only are we concerned about failing, often the concern is connected to whether or not those we minister to will be receptive of what we have to say, especially if they know anything about our past.

Remember, what happened in your past belongs right there; in your past. It can no longer have the effect it had on you when you were engaged in it. You don't have to hate the person you used to be. Embrace the fact that there are some shades of black and grey in the past. If you had not had the 'before salvation' experiences, you wouldn't be as good a witness of the mercy and grace God bestowed upon you. It took everything you went through from birth to the realization of your godly calling to prepare you for the work.

Don't be concerned about your qualifications. The promise you have is greater than any obstacle designed to distract you. You have something in the word of God to hold on to. Hold on to the fact that you know God called you and has a plan for your life. Hold on to the understanding that there is an expected end for you, and the in-between matters. Hold on to the knowledge that the Lord has already equipped you to do the work. Hold on to the blessed hope that He will be with you while you walk it out[19]. Hold on to the grace of His glory to accomplish your purpose. Hold on to the word that He never starts anything that He is not able to finish.[20]

Jesus knew that the call to stand in the gap for sinful men would take Him through dangerous pastures. Knowing this did not deter the obvious obligation of the commission to complete the work. On the way to Calvary He made a detour to the garden at the foot of Mount Olive, called Gethsemane. This garden would be known as a special meeting place for Jesus to talk to His Father. In conversation with the Holy Father, Jesus discussed the desire not to have to endure the pain and torture intended to be inflicted by the same sinful men He was here to save: nonetheless, He realized that there was an intrinsic need to be faithful to see the Father's plan through. Desperate men would need to have something to hold on to when they would find themselves without answers to the most disturbing situations. He left us with the example that we have of God to hold to in times of trouble. His disciples failed to stand with Him in prayer so it was obvious that they were not dependable; but he knew he could hold on to what He knew about the God who entrusted him with enormous purpose.

---

[19]   And, behold, I am with thee, and will keep thee, whithersoever thou goest, and will bring thee again into this land. For I will not leave thee, until I have done that which I have spoken to thee of. (Gen 28:15)

[20]   Being confident of this very thing, that he which hath begun a good work in you will perform it until the day of Jesus Christ: (Php 1:6)

Submit to the Sovereign

Chapter 4 (I Timothy 6:15-16[21])

As Jesus prayed in the garden the Bible declares that He made a profound statement. There was not much to this statement at first glance, but when you understand the defining moment connected to the statement we see the profundity of it. This statement has been reiterated around the world, yet many who have quoted it have misunderstood it in its truest form. While He prayed on behalf of men; some of whom had already been born, and many that were yet to come; He said, "O my Father, if it be possible, let this cup pass from me: nevertheless not as I will, but as thou wilt." (Mat 26:39b)

Jesus now enjoins Himself to purpose. He had not come into the earth to carry a title and be served by men. The very reason for his earthly experience was linked to the journey out. We now see Him in His humanity as never before noticed. No man could possibly imagine himself preparing to die a horrendous death as that of the cross without agonizing over it. He agonized, not over His personal outcome of this occurrence, but rather the circumstances to incur. In this portion of conversation He acknowledges the true human desire that often struggles with the spiritual understanding. We must be honest enough at this juncture to, at the very least, acknowledge that often our spirit-man and our humanity struggle against one another. The dreadful issue of determining to do right and wrong is contingent on whether we give in to the spirit or the flesh which both reside with us. Paul exposes this struggle in the book of Romans when he speaks on the war that takes

---

[21] Which in his times he shall shew, *who is* the blessed and only Potentate, the King of kings, and Lord of lords; Who only hath immortality, dwelling in the light which no man can approach unto; whom no man hath seen, nor can see: to whom *be* honour and power everlasting. Amen. (1Ti 6:15-16)

place in the mind of man. The conclusion of the matter is that we have a choice; whether to follow after and obey the flesh which ultimately leads to eternal death or to walk after the spirit and gain eternal life.

While talking to His Father in the garden, Jesus once again leaves us a significant model to pattern after. Although he was feeling one thing in the flesh, ultimately He yields to the sovereign power of God. In teaching the disciples He made it clear that the Son of man had to allow Himself to be offered as a sacrifice for all of mankind. He knew that even as He would be lead to the slaughter to die, He likewise would be raised up. It would be in the fullness of this process that we could then obtain eternal life. It had already been proven that Jesus was able to raise the dead, even while they had been dead for a few days.[22] Therefore, if there would be a question at this point it might be, "Who then would raise Him up?" Only an All-Powerful God could handle such as awesome task. There is no man born on earth who can raise the dead but Christ, so if He were the one to be raised, it could only be accomplished by someone equally or more powerful than He. Therefore it's safe to conclude that His Father might be powerful enough to do it.

The Father that Jesus spoke to is the same God who stepped out on nothing and called things into existence and brought them to order. His name alone is Jehovah and His is the Most High in all the earth. This is the only wise God, the creator of all the earth, the one who sees all and knows all. Paul points this out to Timothy as he instructs and prepares him to carry out his pastoral ministry. He says to Timothy, "Remember who it is that called you, the one whom you serve and is worthy of your service." We tend to get side-tracked because along the way we seem to forget who our God is. God is not like man; He cannot and will not lie. He is not like our adversary, and is not conniving or underhanded. He is a holy God, a powerful God, a God of truth. We can submit our ways to Him because He has a set plan for us. He is always looking out for us,

---

22   So when Jesus came, he found that he had been in the tomb four days already. Now Bethany was nigh unto Jerusalem, about fifteen furlongs off; (John 11:17-18) And when he had thus spoken, he cried with a loud voice, Lazarus, come forth. He that was dead came forth, bound hand and foot with grave-clothes; and his face was bound about with a napkin. Jesus saith unto them, Loose him, and let him go. (John 11:43-44)

and does what is best for us. What He desires for His children is that we would have the very best. If we would trust Him, even in hard times, we will see that everything we are exposed to or go through works for our good.

If we serve a God with power to bring things into existence simply by speaking it, we can be confident that His plan will work for us. It helps to know that He will never leave you. Any God who cares enough to go into the dungeons of life with you although He is holy can certainly be trusted to keep you in any situation you may find yourself in. Jesus shows us that God can be trusted by His final answer: He says, "I'm not going to strive for my own will; I'll give in to yours." In other words He was willing to forget about His manly desire to walk away and not have to go to the cross, and do it because it was a necessity for the many lives that were at stake. How many times have we had to make such a tough choice to either do what was comfortable or what was necessary. It's comfortable to ask to be excused, but it's necessary to be in place. It's comfortable to call in sick, but it's necessary to go to the meeting and face the music. It's comfortable to sit in the pew, but it's necessary to walk out your calling. It's comfortable to tell everyone else how to straighten out their life, but it's necessary to heed wise council and get your own life straight. God never calls us to do what is comfortable; He calls us to do what is necessary.

Our love for the Lord and desire to please Him should be enough to cause us to give in to His plan for our lives. Jesus was only yielding to the plan that was already in place. God has the power to maneuver us through whatever plan He has for our lives. What you've been selected to accomplish may be a bit much for you to handle alone. That's due to the fact that He not only wants you to give in to His plan, but also to trust him to help you to achieve it. We don't have the power to realize our carnal goals alone. We need God that much more to deal with spiritual opposition. The circumstances Jesus had to face carried a spiritual connotation. Likewise the work we are entrusted to bring about has spiritual implication.

When you walk in the steps that are ordered for you by the sovereign God you must know that He gives those who would dare to do His will supernatural charge of abilities to work with. He enables us to demonstrate the way His mighty power flows through us. To those who do not know Him these capabilities may be astounding persuaders. To those whom He empowers with these faculties, they are provisions to exercise. God is the greatest power; therefore, if we truly trust Him we shouldn't have a problem giving everything to Him. This includes giving up control of our life. Now that's a sore spot of men. Control is the most difficult thing for man to surrender in life. It creates the greatest obstacle. In fact, it is one of the few things we clutch subconsciously.

The Bible declares that, "The steps of a good man are ordered by the Lord." The only way to walk in steps that are sorted out for you is to walk in those steps as opposed to your own. Many of us say we trust God, and want to ultimately become everything He desires us to be here on earth; but few are those who would allow ourselves to be different or strange enough to become that. We are given instructions one at a time, and that without any explanation. Paul says we only know part of any story.[23] So the question is, "Are you willing to do what God says without knowing the full plan?"

Most of us sabotage our own story because we are unwilling to yield control of our lives to a God we know to be Almighty. Our limited understanding of Him is that there is no one and no god who can stand close to Him by measure of strength and might. We agree that He created all things in heaven and in the earth. Yet we lack the faith necessary to stop trying to formulate life to work the way we think it should work. I urge you to let go and let God do what He does best. Much of the trials and calamity you face in your day-to-day struggles are at your own hands, simply because you will not give up the reins so the Lord can guide you through the mazes that lead to the definitive anticipation. The question is, are we prepared to maintain in each realm, as we move from faith to faith.

Given the option and knowing the pain, problems, and promise ahead; how would you answer in the state of affairs Jesus faced? How many of us have learned that God has power to bring us through any circumstance presented to us? Do you have a 'nevertheless' in your prayers? God's people have got to trust Him enough to be honest and

---

[23] For we know in part, and we prophesy in part. (1Co 13:9)

say "I really don't want to do what you're asking me to do." It's alright to tell Him how you actually feel. He wants you to always truthfully state your position, as you cannot deceive, or bamboozle Him. Tell Him, "I don't like the place I'm in right now." Let Him know, "This is too much for me to bear alone." There is no punishment for frankness. Integrity is absolutely necessary for you to operate with the measure of power you already have in you. If you can't be honest with the Lord you can't be trusted to convey the message you must deliver to men with sincerity.

No matter how you feel or what obstacles are presented to you, maintain a spirit that says you're willing to hold on until the end. Yield control of all you have to God and allow Him to guide you through life. Don't give in to the distractions of life that threaten the power of God and His plan for you. Keep your mind and body under subjection to walk in divine favor. Ultimately, don't worry about tomorrow, or the trials that you may have to face. Let the power of the Almighty work in you so you can realize the pinnacle of the plan that's been laid out for you.

You may not understand what God is doing, but just to know He's doing something and it's with you and others you will touch is enough to let Him have control. Even when we have absolutely no idea what the expected outcome is, if we trust God, we know that the good the bad and the indifferent are all working for our advantage.[24] This gives reason to submit. Submission is not the terrible word many people make it out to be. It's not a negative or imprisoning word, and yet it is.

Paul introduced himself as a prisoner of Christ.[25] He's not a prisoner as a means of punishment. The reference here is not to a sentence imposed upon him. He labels himself a prisoner to express his voluntary submission to God's purpose. After his encounter with Jesus on the road to Damascus he set out on a different path from being a persecutor of the people of God, to preaching the gospel to the lost.[26]

---

[24]   And we know that all things work together for good to them that love God, to them who are the called according to *his* purpose. (Rom 8:28)

[25]   For this cause I Paul, the prisoner of Jesus Christ for you Gentiles, (Eph 3:1)

[26]   And straightway he preached Christ in the synagogues, that he is the Son of God. (Act 9:20)

God is not going to force you to walk in His purpose. He's not going to tie you up or bind you in physical chains. He's not going to punish you to get you to do what He wants. After all, the benefit of obedience to the Lord is for you. Paul now sets another example for us in that he gives himself whole-heartedly to the work of the gospel ministry. So what he's saying to us is that we should let God be the captain of our lives. Give yourself to Him completely, not worrying about what other people may say about you or whether or not they are as committed to the gospel ministry. Don't be afraid to be a servant (minister) to others; as you only serve God as well as you serve men.[27]

Although God can do whatever He wants to, He allows us to have the deciding vote in the campaign of our life's direction. We have the option to deliver others as we have been delivered. Someone who witnesses how your salvation changed your life may desire to be saved. Witnessing the move of divine power in your life should whet the pallet of someone who's never known the power of God or what it can accomplish in their life.

---

[27] And the King shall answer and say unto them, Verily I say unto you, Inasmuch as ye have done *it* unto one of the least of these my brethren, ye have done *it* unto me. (Mat 25:40)

Survive the Struggle

Chapter 5 (Hebrews 10:32[28])

As Jesus prayed in the garden, Judas came with the Roman soldiers to apprehend Him. This was the beginning of the end of His days here on earth. Jesus already knew what the rest of the world would soon discover. Before arriving at this pivotal moment, Jesus had been in discussion (prayer) with the one who sent Him. In the midst of conversation He had asked a vital question that would reveal to us an answer so pertinent to the life of every Christian and their assignment here on earth. The question He had asked His Father was directly tied to events that would soon follow this encounter. When we realize the call on our lives to serve, we don't know as much as He did. We actually struggle more with that which we do not know rather than that which we know.

Jesus struggled with the knowledge that He would soon endure a most horrific situation not for punishment, but for purpose. Many men had stood before the justice system to be found guilty of some crime, then were remanded to suffer the consequences of their actions. The suffering they faced would fit the offense or crime that was committed. If found to be a thief, the culprit might suffer to have a finger or hand chopped off. If the transgression was more serious it wasn't strange that they might be put to death by one method or another. The law required any offender to be punished according to the offense. The issue concerning the suffering of Christ brings to the forefront the true imperfections of the law. If the law had been perfect, how could it allow a man who had done no wrong to hang on a cross between two who had offended it. So when He expressed the preference for the cup to be removed, He

---

28   But call to remembrance the former days, in which, after ye were illuminated, ye endured a great fight of afflictions; (Heb 10:32)

already knew that although it was possible it would not have brought about God's desired end.

The writer of Hebrews brings a couple of interesting points to us in the 32nd verse of chapter ten in his quest to encourage the readers to consider how to deal with the trials we may face on our way to fulfilling godly purpose. He reminds us that if we have relationship with God, it first entails a history. Utilizing historical references enables us to see how we came through one situation and to understand the possibility to survive whatever we are enduring in life at this very moment. Once we were enlightened to know that Jehovah does indeed exist and is not a fictitious character, allowing Him to show Himself in power and glory, we were put in position to meet the challenge of opposition. There are many people in this world who doubt the very existence of the living God. These, as well as some who profess to believe in Him often may wreak havoc in your life, intentionally or accidentally.

Opposition comes with many faces. Everyone who knows that you operate in ministry is not ecstatic about it. In fact, some of the very people you think should be supportive of your decision to give in to the prodding of God will be the ones first in line to speak against you. Our trepidation to do the will of God is often instigated by our apprehension concerning what people know about us and what affect that will have on their ability to receive the gospel we are called to preach. Those who knew you when may still hold your past in the forefront of their minds, hindering their ability to accept the metamorphosis you passed through. This could present some challenges as you move forward in ministry. Maybe in your past you hung out in the party scene, smoking drinking, and exercising promiscuity. It could be that you were strung out on drugs, or worse still, a functional addict moving through society as though everything was normal. You could have been a pimp or a prostitute. Whatever is in your past that people try to use to ignore the word of God spoken through you can be overcome as your walk with God changes the way you live. When others witness the difference your relationship with the Lord has made in your life, it will convince them to allow Him to effect change in their life. Whatever you have done in the past is not a disqualifier of your future exploits with God. They have no place in the determination of your pursuit to please God by obedience to His will. Don't let the apprehensions and misgivings of others determine whether you follow after the destiny charted out for you. Walk in the will of God, no matter the level of discomfort you may have to bear. Paul said we should go through hard times with the enduring abilities of soldiers going to war.[29]

A struggle speaks of a fight or resistance. Many of us who profess our love toward God have fought against making changes we thought to be uncomfortable although we realize it is necessary for the sake of the kingdom. We seem to choose comfort for our own sake over life changing challenges that will affect our witness to others. Your issue may be letting go of some habit, or person you are content to have around. It could be yielding to an expectation or call that may bring about unfamiliar changes in your life. Maybe you are fearful about what others may think of you.

I recall saying to the Lord, "God who is going to listen to me? Most of the people around me are always trying to prove that they are just as good as I am at just about anything. Many of the people in my church talk about me behind my back. I don't think even my family members think very much of me. I don't know that much about the Bible or how to share what's in it. What am I going to say?" He assured me once again by telling me not to pay attention to the expression on other peoples' faces, and just learn how to hear from Him so I could articulate what He tells me to say.

I struggled with my past, with what others knew about it, and the idea that it could somehow affect my capability to develop a lasting viable relationship with God, much less my capacity to communicate the gospel to draw men to Him. I realize that the reason many people are not successful is because they lack the ability to survive the struggle and walk out the divine will of the Lord as a witness of His favor. This brought another concern to mind. What or who might this struggle be with? The answer is that we struggle first with God about the authenticity of the call we believe we have on our life. You should seek to be certain that it is indeed the voice of God you're hearing or the prodding coming from Him you feel. The greatest thing a person can do is move in the

---

[29]   Thou therefore endure hardness, as a good soldier of Jesus Christ. (2Ti 2:3)

vein of divine calling. The worst thing one could do is operate outside of God's will or calling.

It is imperative that we win the battle within in order to please God. No one on earth knows as much about you as you know about yourself. The only one who is always with you, and knows the thoughts you think is you. Whatever back room or dark alley you've been in, others may or may not know about, but you were there. You were there when you did what you did, with whomever you did it, wherever you did it. You know what you were thinking when you were entangled in ungodly habits. You know every conversation, or negative thought you had about that someone who may not have thought the best of you either. There is none other who could hold you back and keep you from your true destiny like you but you.

The greatest struggle any man has to overcome is the struggle within. God may instruct you to speak, but only you can take the action of speaking. He may tell you to go someplace, but you have to make the effort to go. He may desire you to preach, but you have to open your mouth and preach the word. No one can do what you are commanded to do for the sake of the body of Christ out of obedience to the almighty will of God for you. You have to make it through the struggle that tells you that you are not qualified. You have to fight your way through the lack of esteem that may be a hindrance. You must hear the word of God over anyone who would dare try to tell you that you have no message. No matter what you used to be, you have to stand against what is not in the will of God. You have to develop courage to stand strong in the power and anointing that only comes from above. You must be determined to win over any element that would dare make any attempt to stop you from reaching a place of purpose. You have to know that the purpose in your life is more powerful than anything that would discourage it. Above all, know that God has the ability and authority to give you victory in any circumstance you may find yourself beleaguered with.

Jesus knew that the only way He could make it through the courthouse railroads, cat-tail beating, crowd screaming, spitting, name calling, misinterpretations, misunderstanding, etc, was to win first the battle within. He asked that the cup, filled with all of these antics would be removed from Him, but the winning coin was the one that had the most powerful word a child of God needs to know. This word outweighs the most mind-boggling scientific theory. This word has the power to untangle much chemical atomic relativity. One word can change the course of life, and cause you to overcome hesitation so you can fulfill your destiny. Jesus renders the ultimate example for us by saying. "'Nevertheless', not my will but your will be done." It is the 'nevertheless' that catapults Him into the divine purpose that brought Him to earth. His mission could not be fulfilled without the 'nevertheless' in His vocabulary.

We all should have this powerful word in our arsenal. It's alright to tell God how you feel about going through an uncomfortable situation. He doesn't mind hearing that you don't really want to have to endure a painful state of affairs. The most honorable thing you could do is be perfectly honest with Him. It has been instilled in so many of our lives that we should not question God, leading us to believe that He is not interested in how we really feel. The truth of the matter is that our feelings are not going to change whether or not we must go through humiliation, yet He does want us to tell Him about it. Although telling Him won't necessarily change the course of events, it speaks of our understanding of His character. We should recognize that we can be totally honest with God. This awareness helps us to move beyond our feelings and ultimately submit to His strategy. God can do anything, even the extraordinary through an obedient child, and He will demonstrate Himself through you over and over.

It's not unusual for a woman to struggle with whether or not to go through with a pregnancy; especially when extenuating circumstances are involved. Women have contemplated what to do in many instances for decades. Often the unfortunate need has presented itself to consider if a woman should give birth to the product of a rape, or abusive relationship. Some have chosen not to put themselves in position to be constantly reminded of the abusive person while raising their child: However there are those who made the decision that although the situation was not ideal, the baby would still be an emblem of God's amazing love for us. These women operate out of the need as well as the desire to survive any obstacle through the spirit and power of the sovereign God.

Statement of Success

Chapter 6 (I Chronicles 28:20[30])

The world equates success much differently than God. If we were to assess a battle, the victor would be considered the one who defeated the opposition, enabling them to stand towering powerfully above them. Anyone the world deems successful would be the one living high, the one having authority over others who then serve them. Immediate observation of the enduring slaughter of Christ would leave the impression that He definitely was not victorious.

How could a man who lost a case in court with no evidence against him be supposed victorious? How could a man be whipped all night long with glass and nails tied to leather bands and still be considered successful? What man could be forced to carry the weapon to be used to the place of assassination and still be reckoned a success? When Jesus hung His head and gave up the ghost, it couldn't have possibly been thought that He was successful. He didn't even have His own tomb to be buried in. This doesn't seem at all to be a successful man: yet we know Him to be the most successful man to ever walk the earth.

David shared some awesomely powerful advice with his son Solomon. If you are looking to be successful this advice must resonate in your mind from time to time. David had established a new system, founded upon grace as its principle at the time of appointing Solomon to the throne and changes the age for the Levites to commence to their godly service. (Darby, 1979) This is actually a continuation of the conversation he had

---

[30] And David said to Solomon his son, Be strong and of good courage, and do *it:* fear not, nor be dismayed: for the LORD God, *even* my God, *will be* with thee; he will not fail thee, nor forsake thee, until thou hast finished all the work for the service of the house of the LORD. (1Ch 28:20)

begun in the ninth verse of the 28th chapter of 1st Chronicles by telling his son to know God for himself. He knew the importance of personal relationship all too well. David had already established his relationship and had seen the results; so passing this on to his son would be valuable in what he would have to face as king of Israel. Solomon would need to be willing to serve God with pureness of heart, not simply out of duty or ceremony. Jehovah is one who looks beyond facial expression. He doesn't rely on words that come out of our mouths. He searches for the pureness that is only expressed from our heart. He understands the thoughts and imaginations that men see as mysterious. He tells him that God will reveal Himself to anyone who searches for Him in His divinity.

David's conversation now turns to motivation from relationship. He should be motivated by the history of relationship developed with God. Because he has a point of reference, he knows he can trust God with anything. He tells his son to be strong: don't give in to weakness. Do not allow the flesh to prevail over the spirit. Stand firm in what he believes and do it with courage. The enemy tries to make us turn away from what we know about God. The statement 'be strong' speaks of exhibiting power, while 'courage' tells of one who is alert, agile, and energetic. Those of us who would be successful must not only be strong; but attentive, responsive, and tough. These are not cowards' characteristics. You cannot serve God in fullness if you are afraid to do what He tells you.

God cannot send you anywhere that He will not be with you. In His omnipresence, you can trust that he is always with you. David says now that God will be there until the work is finished. He is a God who finishes whatever He starts. Not only did Solomon need these encouraging words, but we who are chosen to do the work of the Lord have to remember that He is unable to fail. Whatever He says, it will come to pass: we can trust His word, no matter how far-fetched it sounds. Be attentive to hear the word God speaks for your life, it will happen. Don't try to fit Him in your box, expand yourself to His universe. Know that He is with you wherever you go. He is the same God who was in the pit, then the prison with Joseph; and brought him out to sit in the palace. He is the same God who was with Abraham on the mountain, and even in the land that he was unfamiliar with. David said He would be with you from the darkest condition to the brightest expression.[31]

God can get success out of anything. He can bring the lowliest of men or the most sinful woman to boardroom status. To be a statement of God's success you don't have to be wealthy. You don't have to possess the highest degree from the most noted school. You don't have to come from a world famous family. You don't have to be the most talented or the best looking person. All it takes to be successful is a desire to win. The desire to win gives one reason to hold out until the end: and there lies the one who is victorious. True victory does not come from landing on the top of the heap-pile, it comes from landing.

While it didn't appear that Jesus was triumphant when He died for our sins, or when He was buried in the tomb, inevitably there was victory. It was realized as He conquered death, hell, and the grave. It was realized when He arose on the third day. It was understood as He appeared to His disciples. We know He won because we now have a right to eternal life. Just as Jesus won the victory over sin and satan by dying and being raised up for our sakes, we can be triumphant by finishing the course that was set for us.

When you go through hard trials, remember you must finish your course. When you face opposition keep in mind that you need to finish your course. When family and friends forsake you, press your way to finish your course. When you don't understand why you have to go through what you have to go through, reason to finish your course. Your victory isn't in when you reach the finish line, it is only that you finish.

Jesus was compelled to finish His mission by what He already knew and in turn, exhibited a most essential example in facing traumatic experiences associated with our purpose. He remained focused on the intention of

---

[31]   Whither shall I go from thy spirit? or whither shall I flee from thy presence? If I ascend up into heaven, thou *art* there: if I make my bed in hell, behold, thou *art there*. *If* I take the wings of the morning, *and* dwell in the uttermost parts of the sea; Even there shall thy hand lead me, and thy right hand shall hold me. (Psa 139:7-10)

His charge. It was crucial that He would finish the undertaking. There was so much more at stake than just His own life. So many souls yet to be born were in dire need, and had Jesus not followed through with what was ahead, they would be lost. If Jesus hadn't gone through with the fullness of His mission, we would not now have access to eternal life. Although Jesus was confronted with a tough decision at His weakest moment, the utmost consideration could not be associated with what He was feeling at that moment.

In that instance Jesus made His decision based on how it would affect not Him, not just the Jewish nation, but also those of us who would be born of a different pedigree and in a different age. In this, He exemplifies the standard by which we should base our decision. Jesus surmised that it was not optional to quit. If He had allowed immediate circumstances to govern His choice, souls would be lost. Although it was going to be exuberantly painful to be beaten, then carry a heavy cross up a mountainside with open wounds only to be nailed to it, it still had to be done. While He knew He was the messiah yet the only accolades would be the derogatory names He would be called by those who did not understand the magnitude of His suffering. The right decision was crucial. Because of the sensitivity associated with this awesome assignment, Jesus' first decision was that He didn't actually have a choice.

Jesus had already declared that He only came to do the work that His Father had assigned; therefore there was no choice to be made. Instead of trying to find a loophole or a way out, Jesus gives the ultimate response that He would still go forth with the mission. He knows that historical records show Jehovah to be able to bring His people through anything. This enables Him now to say, "O my Father, if this cup may not pass away from me, except I drink it, thy will be done."[32] At this point angels ministered to Him, giving Him the strength needed to complete the work. God will dispatch angels to give you the grace and strength necessary to finish whatever He has instructed you to accomplish. In order to cash

---

[32] He went away again the second time, and prayed, saying, O my Father, if this cup may not pass away from me, except I drink it, thy will be done. (Mat 26:42)

in on the grace and strength you have to yield completely to His will, without consideration of your immediate condition.

The purpose within you is to be developed, birthed, and nurtured, not aborted. Stay connected and focused on who the Lord called you to be. Let Him work through you to bring you to your expected end. There is no greater measure of success than reaching a place of expectation and be met with the blessings of the Lord. If you understand that your God-assigned tasks are not just about you and make the decision to go through whatever you will in the process of fulfilling the work should trigger your choice to do what's right above what feels good. What's satisfying is not equivalent to what is successful. We have to follow through with our purpose, not without thought of giving up but without doing so, that our success might save others.

It stands to reason that so many women may have cheated themselves of the wonder of raising highly successful children by aborting them. This is not to mention the fact that these children were cheated out of the opportunity to rise to the top and make great accomplishments. Unfortunately while there is such strong concentration on the struggle attached to mental and emotional distress, it overwhelms all possible expectations of achievement so many parents take pleasure in. Trust God for all things no matter the circumstances associated with what you're facing. Make the decision to believe in His sovereignty and know that there is a plan for your life to walk you into a place of victory.

Paul spoke of the overwhelming power of God as he wrote in the third chapter of the book of Ephesians, "Now unto him that is able to do exceeding abundantly above all that we ask or think, according to the power that worketh in us, (Eph 3:20). I found that although God is all-powerful, and has done much for us, there are some things He has never done.

Things God has never done:

- Started a project He couldn't finish (Left a work undone)
- Walked out on His children
- Met an opponent He couldn't conquer
- Seen a storm He could not control

- Faced a problem He could not solve
- Heard a question He could not answer
- Asked us to do anything for Him that He wouldn't do for us
- Given up on us

In this we should find a renewed sense of strength and courage so you won't give up on God. You might find that it's not so easy to walk away from your true purpose in life. True purpose follows you. Today you may walk away, but somewhere down the line it will catch up to you. Many signs will follow you like sleepless nights, dreams and visions about the very gift you never used. The farther you get off course, the more you will long to be where God desires you to be. Pull out that nevertheless tucked in the recesses of your spirit; nurture and develop the gifts God has placed inside of you. Move into the birthing position, and prepare to press on to your purpose and destiny.

You may have to go by way of crucifixion, but you can't stop. You may have to be completely reformed, but if a seed doesn't fall and die it will not be able to bring forth anything prolific. You may have to go by way of darkness, but you must go through with it in order to make it to the light. You may lose some things, but you have far more to gain. You may have to deal with temporary discomfort, but it will be worth it all when you behold the abundance of love and favor the Lord blesses you with.

Somebody needs to hear the powerful word of God out of your mouth. Someone needs to see the release of the anointing you have paid for with sweat, tears, and trials of life. Somebody needs to receive deliverance by the gift within you. Someone needs to grab on to the visionary guidance as you hear from God.

God's chosen vessels cannot afford to be spiritual dropouts. We must fulfill every dream, vision, and promised word dwelling within us. Every word He has spoken concerning us must come to pass in the earth. Allow the Lord to complete the work through you. Go through the process, follow His directives, and let His will be done in your life. Don't abort, but give birth to your purpose, then walk it out to reach your place of destiny. The path to the throne takes us through experiences in the pit of despair, onto the house of deception, and to the deepest dungeons of darkness. It's not where you go but how you travel that will determine your definitive destination.

Hold on to the word of God as you submit to His sovereign will. Realize that as you reach full-term, He is the attending physician who ultimately delivers us through the trials and tribulations of life to win our greatest conquest.

Works Cited

Amplified Bible. (1987). The Lockman Foundation.

The American Heritage® Dictionary of the English Language: Fourth Edition. 2000.

1769 King James Authorized Version Bible (KJV) Red Letter Edition

www.ingramcontent.com/pod-product-compliance
Lightning Source LLC
Chambersburg PA
CBHW061222280526
45784CB00006B/2599